HAVENS

An Intimate Collection Of Exclusive Photographs

Of Celebrities And Their Favorite Rooms

By

Michael McCreary

Introduction By

Whoopi Goldberg

To David,

my brother,

my friend, my inspiration.

*W*ith love and heartfelt appreciation to the following individuals and companies, without whose talent, generosity, care and support, this book would not have been possible.

Assistant Photographer

ART GRAY

Stylists

MARLENA DICTOR

JIM WALTERS

KRISTINE SILVERMAN

BRIAN TOFFOLI

KIMBER KLUSMAN

Graphic Designers

JOHN JOHNSON

LORI LEBOY

Hair & Make-up Artists

DAVID MIRAMONTES

CARREY GIBBONS

KAREN SCALES

DAVID SIEBENALER

BRIDGETT BALLOU

Executive Producer

DONALD WAYNE

Producer

AVA FARENTINO

*S*ponsors

MICHAEL FOSS

ALAN HAMEL

SUZANNE SOMERS

ALLAN JEFFRIES FRAMING CENTER	TOBY & NANCY ILAND
JAMIE & POLLY ANDERSON	JERRY MABA
FRED BOCK MUSIC CO. INC.	BARRY PEELE
STERLING CLARK	TOM PETERS
MICHAEL DEGAETANO	CARL ROMEO
DR. ALLYSON B. FRIED/PODIATRIST	ART SPAETH
JAY FUJITANI	TOM SWALE

Company Services

DENNIS HOLAHAN

JOEL SAMUELS/PHOTORUN

IRENA'S PHOTOGRAPHIC
RENTAL SERVICES

A & I PRINTS

DAVID CHANG/SUPER COLOR LAB

JED/SD COLOR

RITA FLORA

PRESTON DAVIS WEST

INNER GARDENS

JAMES COX/WALTER ALLEN PLANT RENTALS

JILL ROBERTS . . . ETHEREAL

WILCOPY PRINTERS

FIORI/FLORALLY DISTINCTIVE

OMEGA/CINEMA PROPS

BOUNTIFUL

FREWIL DESIGNS

CENTINELA FEED & PET SUPPLY

PROPS SERVICES WEST

JACKSON SHRUB SUPPLY, INC.

SAMY'S CAMERA

SUNSET PHOTO LAB

BLUEPRINT

SPECIAL THANKS

TED & ANNETT SHACKELFORD

MARK PIERSON

*To all the celebrities and their families who cared enough to open their homes,
and to their personal assistants and their public relation firms.*

ACKNOWLEDGMENTS

John Aaroe, Jennifer Allen, Peter Anthony, Terri Aronson, Avjet, Joe Babajian, Robin Baum, Barbara Benvil, Marjorie Anne Bernard, Brad Bessy, Jim Blevins, Stephen Block, David Burnham, Brad Cafarelli, Gary Campbell, Kevin Campbell, Kathy Carey, Kevin Carlisle, Lil Chain, Antonia Coffman, Jeff Collins, Kim Conant, Daneen Conroy, Judy Cycon, Ray Danner, Freddy & Candy DeMann, Susan Dubow, Marge Duncan, Ed Fabian, Tony Farentino, Ed Fitz, Michael Foss, Dottie Galliano, Bernice Gershon, Jill Greenbaum, Jeff Greenberg, Ron Hacker, Sheila Hanahan, James Hancock, Erick Huff, Felix Iturraran, Jerry Jackson, Jack Jason, Shawn Kadivics, Dan Karslake, Lisa Kasteler, Elizabeth Keener, John Kirby, Peter Levinson, Erin Mahon, Delphine Mann, Linda Marder, Tony Marinelli, Grant Matthews, Rick Millikan, Tom Nelson, Rod Olstrom, Outline, Paragon Photo, Bret Parsons, Mark Peterson, John Rainbow, Chris Reynolds, Cork & Mary Rugroden, Wallace Seawell, Kim Silva, Malcom Smith, Catherine Sodi, Don Spradlin, Rick Stockwell, Susan Such, Armen Sultanian, Rich Thurber, Lisa Todd, Robert Trachtenberg, Shelly Willner, Annett Wolf, Elizabeth Wright, Marsha Yanchuck, Gregory Zarian, Paul Ziert and *anyone else who helped us in any way with this project.*

Publisher: W. Quay Hays
Managing Editor: Colby Allerton
Copy Editor: Peter Hoffman
Production Director: Nadeen Torio
Color and Prepress Director: Gaston Moraga

For information:
General Publishing Group, Inc.
2701 Ocean Park Boulevard
Santa Monica, CA 90405

Library of Congress Catalog Card Number 95-077224

Printed in Italy
10 9 8 7 6 5 4 3 2 1

General Publishing Group
Los Angeles

Table of Contents

WHOOPI GOLDBERG	11	JEFF GOLDBLUM	70
TIMOTHY STEELE	13	MARSHA MASON	72
JOHNNY MATHIS	14	PENNY MARSHALL	74
DEMI MOORE	16	GARRY MARSHALL	76
LEEZA GIBBONS	18	DONNA MILLS	78
PHYLLIS DILLER	20	BARBARA BAIN	80
SUSAN ANTON	22	BART SIMPSON	82
NADIA COMANECI	24	DIONNE WARWICK	84
BART CONNER	24	NICOLAS CAGE	86
ANN-MARGRET	26	ANNETTE FUNICELLO	88
HENRY MANCINI	28	ROSEANNE	90
SANDY DUNCAN	30	THERESA SALDANA	92
SUZANNE SOMERS	32	MARIETTE HARTLEY	94
SALLY KELLERMAN	34	DEIDRE HALL	96
JUDITH LIGHT	36	HARRY HAMLIN	98
ELVIRA	38	HOWIE MANDEL	100
RUE McCLANAHAN	40	DEBBIE REYNOLDS	102
MARIANNE WILLIAMSON	42	BRUCE JENNER	104
MARLEE MATLIN	44	SHIRLEY MacLAINE	106
BARRY MANILOW	46	TERI GARR	108
DONNA PESCOW	48	KENNY G	110
LESLEY ANN WARREN	50	CAROL CHANNING	112
BARBARA EDEN	52	"EDDIE", MOOSE	114
ROBERT HAYS	54	FRANK GEHRY	116
CLIVE BARKER	56	MARK JACKSON	118
LINDA GRAY	58	MICHELE LEE	120
MELISSA ETHERIDGE	60	CHERYL TIEGS	122
JIM LAMPLEY	62	JAMES FARENTINO	124
BREE WALKER	62	TERI HATCHER	126
CLORIS LEACHMAN	64	SHIRLEY JONES	128
TED SHACKELFORD	66	RICK ALLEN	130
LAURA DERN	68	JOHN TRAVOLTA	132

A room that says "glad to see you" is a room to brag about. It embraces every part of your soul. It's that room that lets you be you and enjoy it.

It's where you hang with friends or lovers, moms or dads, dogs, cats, pot-bellied pigs and little kids.

Come on in and see where people go when they want to be somewhere wonderful.

WHOOPI GOLDBERG

HAVENS

The sparrows hunt for seeds in grass still wet,
Commuting to the yard from no great distance.
Some perch on wires, stropping beaks as if
They'd barbered in a previous existence,
While others, in the birdbath, splash and fluff
Less in a spirit of companionship
Than in a keenly rivalrous toilette
That makes the basin over-spill and drip.

They have their havens by instinctive trust:
Whenever they are threatened or distressed
They scatter to a hedge's leafy haunts,
A cup of grass sufficing for a nest.
Obliged for a more personal response
To anxiety or trouble, we repair
To rooms which, to provide real refuge, must
Be shaped by curiosity and care.

Hence picturing such places calls to mind
Not a sad figure inwardly withdrawn,
But one, say, in a study who prefers
To note the cheerful riot on the lawn,
Who watches sparrows through binoculars
Or locates an old field guide on the shelves
To guess at different species as they feed,
Skim, scutter, dip, and chase among themselves.

Timothy Steele

T love this room for its tranquility. It gives you a feeling of

being outdoors. On a rainy day you can sit by a comfortable

fire in the fireplace and contemplate a swim in the pool. It can

be lively or relaxing. Over the past 30 some years it's been perfect

for all occasions.

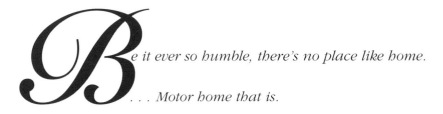

*B*e it ever so humble, there's no place like home.

. . . Motor home that is.

*A*t certain times of the day when the sun is setting it's
almost as if time stands still in our living room. Even

the children seem to wear halos when they're in here . . .

which isn't often, because this is where mommy and daddy

go for "time out."

*T*he very first home was the kitchen. It was a cave. It wasn't much but a protective "haven" til they got fire. Then food started becoming important and had aroma. Raw food doesn't make you get down on your knees and beg.

One of my favorite things to do is to cook. I love to fix food and garnish it creatively and serve it lovingly, by candlelight at night or out-of-doors during the day.

I open the mail in the kitchen because my desk is too messy. My beau and I play cards in the kitchen. My children love to eat with me in the kitchen while we gossip and laugh uproariously and wish we could share our exuberance with the world.

*W*ell, we're newly married so . . . the bedroom of course! We sleep here, we eat here, we read here and we watch T.V. here. We do just about anything you can imagine here. Yes, that's right . . . anything!

*W*e love this room . . . . Well, actually, the entire house is just one room.

It's a really fun place to hang around. After all, we are *a couple of gymnasts.*

*O*f all the rooms in our home, the living room is our favorite. For me, it was necessary to help create a room that was warm yet cheerful, elegant yet cozy . . . a room for family and friends. It is full of treasured gifts from loved ones as well as paintings and family pictures. This is indeed a most happy and comfortable room.

*T*he focal spot for frequent Mancini family gatherings
is our kitchen / family room. Its cozy ambiance reflects the

charm of a small country French restaurant one discovers by

accident that provides unexpected gastronomic delights.

*M*any hours are spent in our family/game room with our boys. This is a place to just hang out, whether it's pool, pinball, listening to music on the juke box or simply relaxing eating popcorn and watching a good movie. It's the room where Don and I can go to feel like kids again.

Other than the laundry, we've done everything else in our kitchen.

*W*e all love this room, my office, because when I'm rehearsing my music I can look out the window and see the children playing in our beautiful yard. They run in and out, occasionally grabbing the microphone to sing eight bars or to play the piano. Whenever daddy has a break from his office next door, he wanders over to sit in the easy chair and gaze out the window and watch everything that's going on. We feel grateful to have such a lovely home . . . so do our bankers.

*I*n our business, the line between personal and professional becomes very vague, and this room reflects that. Our managers have become our family and this is where we can meet, screen our television projects, read or just retreat. It is a sanctuary for all of us—individually and collectively.

call this room "the cave." Pretty creative, huh? It's the one room in my house where I can hang out and really be me. It's dark, creepy and the waterfall outside the window gives it that damp, musty feeling I crave. And talk about impressing your friends . . . just break out the ol' shackles and it's a party!

*F*or the first time I put together a room strictly to please myself, with elements from different areas of my life. Its underlying feel is Southwest, with hand-tooled furniture from Mexico by Allan France and lots of plants and trees with stuffed animals peeking out from them. I added primitive masks and carved statues and totems from Indonesia, Brazil, New Guinea and Mexico, a couple of pieces of my own colored pen drawings, some wonderful dance sticks made by my son, Mark Bish, and a marvelous collection of Beatrice Wood pottery and sculpture, along with a few prehistoric pieces. It's a happy, personal room and it makes me smile.

I spend most of my time in this room. It's where I retreat. In addition to the more obvious things, I also spend a lot of time here playing Candyland, glued to C-Span, reading everything that's hot for the pre-K set, writing as many letters that I don't send as those I do and watching my daughter pretend she's Mariah Carey. I travel a lot of places, but nowhere as much as I travel around while I'm in this room. If there's a physical doorway to my inner life, this is it.

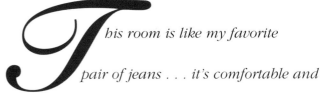 *his room is like my favorite pair of jeans . . . it's comfortable and my husband Kevin and I always have fun in it.*

I *grew up in a tenement apartment in Brooklyn,*

New York, that had a view of the building next

door. I always promised myself that someday I would

build myself a room with a view.

My music studio hangs out over a mountain in Bel Air

and has floor-to-ceiling windows with nothing but

breathtaking views.

I spend as much time here as I can, surrounded by

green mountains, sky and making the music that I

love. I still have to pinch myself every now and

then to believe it's all real.

*W*hen people notice the peanut butter

and jelly stains on the furniture, we

can distract them with the breathtaking view.

In the daytime it becomes a playroom for Jack,

but at night with a roaring fire it becomes a

playroom for Arnold and I.

*T*his is my favorite secret "Lesley" room. It has all

the things that I love: tons of pictures of my son,

my husband-to-be, my mom, my animals and all my

friends. My dolls live in here, my books, a beautiful

deco writing desk . . . it's a comfy place to curl up with

a tea tray and a book. It's where I can be alone for a

moment surrounded by love.

*W*hat I've discovered is that some of the strangest things are romantic. For example, Jon and I frequently prepare meals together, and when you're in love, even that can constitute a romantic evening.

*C*herie has taken a room that seemed separate from the

house and made it an integral part of our home.

A warm place for Christmas, birthdays and special gatherings

full of love and family.

This is the room where I write my books and screenplays. It's a room for dreaming with my eyes open; a room for looking at the sky and seeing other worlds. I've never had a working space I love as much as this room.

A haven for my heart.

*B*y day, this room always feels so sunny and warm. At night, we light candles and our friends gather around the piano for a "hootenanny," singing and playing music until all hours.

*T*he room is the fulfillment of a childhood fantasy for Bree, who grew up in Austin, Minnesota but always thought she should be living in the jungle.

Our four children, two of mine, one of Bree's, one of ours, each chose an animal for the mural. Then the two adult children in the family filled out the menagerie.

When all the kids are playing in here and the room gets really noisy, the parrot screeches, the monkey shrieks and the elephant roars. Seriously! We promise.

My mother used to say, "If you can't fix it, just paint it soft grey-green and put a pot of ivy on it!" So when my Chinese water jug with a brass spigot fell off the iron stand and smashed during the earthquake, I took her advice.

This was a workout room gone wrong. As they were framing the sauna my daughter Dinah glanced in and said, "You know you're never going to use this Mom," and I said, "You're absolutely right." So as the workmen were hoisting a 20-foot beam I said, "Wait! Could you move that out three more feet and put in skylights?" That, French doors and a brick floor . . . and voila . . . a garden room.

This is the part of the house where we spent the first twelve days of our relationship, and it remains the place where we find one another.

T love being in my dressing room,

listening to music, playing dress-up and

cuddling our dog. I enjoy being a girl!

 *his is my favorite room because it's my plaaaaaaayroom.*

*W*hether it's day or night, this room welcomes
you in to view the view, read, contemplate and enjoy.

*T*his is the bedroom of my grandson.

That in itself makes it my favorite room.

*M*any women dream of beautiful homes, expensive jewelry or fancy cars. My wife dreamed of having her own bathroom. She wanted to take bubble baths. A few years ago I had the good fortune to direct the film "Pretty Woman," and after that "bubble bath" scene, I could afford to give my wife her dream. Her bathroom is our favorite room because it makes her happy, and when she's happy I'm happy. We both hang out there during our double bubble bath moments.

I love this room because it's where all my friends gather to share a warm fire, good food and wine and interesting conversation. It's the heart of my home and Chloe and I spend a lot of time here.

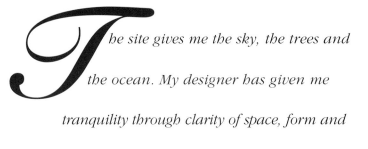

The site gives me the sky, the trees and the ocean. My designer has given me tranquility through clarity of space, form and color. My eye is pleased at every encounter.

*H*ey, man, you gotta admit, my dream bedroom is the coolest hangout in the universe. I did have to put in a lot of fantasizing to bring it up to basic space-age bachelor pad standards. I added various peepholes, a wall safe, trap doors, a pneumatic escape hatch and an anti-matter chamber. It even had a fully functioning kitchenette, perfect for entertaining, but Marge made me get rid of it when she discovered the mice.

1 Midnight observatory tower with mega-powered intergalactic telescope
2 Personal portrait painted by the most brilliant artist of the 20th century
3 Chart of alien life forms
4 Private basketball court
5 Push-button automatic wardrobe selector
6 Complete audiovisual home entertainment center featuring Krusty Channel cable hookup
7 Model planes' dogfight
8 Personal fridge stocked with junk food
9 Video Dream Recorder
10 Miniature heavy-metal-band alarm clock
11 $E=MC^2$ Freeze-Time snooze control
12 Breakfast Butler and Midnight Snack Maid robots
13 Parent-proof bedroom security door
14 Little sister advance detection system
15 See-through wall containing giant ant farm
16 Thumbprint-identifying entrance locks
17 Tattoo machine
18 Glow-in-the-dark blanket
19 Plastic see-through waterbed with live piranhas
20 Tinkle-Matic™ bed-wetting early warning system
21 Secret dungeon
22 Desk that does your homework for you
23 Trap door to tiger cage below
24 Security hounds outside 2 1/2-foot-thick lead door
25 Complete Radioactive Man comic library with professional celebrity wrestler bedtime readers

*T*here are many rooms in my

home I consider "comfy."

My living room denotes just that.

A room to feel comfortable

enough to do what you see me

doing. However, please note

that this privilege is only mine.

My "red room" reminds me of London and my friends can smoke in here.

his has been my home for 30 years. It's not the largest of the

rooms, but it's my favorite. It has such warmth and great meaning

because of all the memorabilia, photos and the piano I played as a

child. I decorated this room in my favorite color, lavender. The teddy

bears are like my children, but my husband, Glen, is the largest of all.

I love the living room in our house because it's a place where we can go and relax, and feel like ourselves. There are pictures of our family, some great ones of the kids, and there's a big cathedral window where the sun can stream through. The whole room has a very warm and comforting feeling to it. Also, there's a grand piano that we all gather around and sing revolting show tunes until we pass out.

*T*he bedroom is the one place where everyone can really relax.

The white wicker is simple and soothing. We've been doing "family

bed" since Tianna was born, so we love our California king-size bed.

It's big enough for all of us to sleep, read, cuddle and play in. For me,

the bedroom is our family's great escape.

There are very few places where I can find total peace. This room is one of them. It is green, my favorite color, and designed by my husband Patrick for after-dinner quiet moments. However, I have stolen it for meditational moments.

It is filled with an eclectic mixture of furnishings rich with their own memories and history. The bed, bought in Paris, is 19th Century Vietnamese. It is made from bamboo shoots and rice straw. The portrait is of Pat's grandmother painted by Stella Mertens, who also happened to be Renoir's model. The hand-carved table, a family heirloom, is French from the late 18th Century with a malachite top.

When I sit in this room I receive an energy and a sense of serenity that I take with me wherever I go. This is indeed a "haven;" a safe harbor; a room of quiet joy.

*T*call this room my "snuggery." The walls are upholstered in

floral chintz, which screens out sounds of a bustling household

and protects my toddler son, David Atticus, as I watch him take

his first steps. When I'm curled up with a good book on the matching

love seat, I feel like I'm sitting in a jewel box. My husband, Steve,

always said I'd wind up in a padded room.

T his room is like a prism to me with so many different

spaces and views. It's an architectural womb where I can

meditate and transcend the Hollywood reality.

A *s a child, I couldn't wait to*

grow up and have my bedroom

decorated my way. Before I had any

success my wife and I slept in my car.

. . . Some things never change.

I love my den because it is so peaceful. I go there to read and

have tranquil thoughts. I open the French doors and look into my

beautiful backyard. It's a comfort zone.

*I*t's a lot of fun working out as a family and we

both like keeping our bodies in shape for each

other. It's fabulous to have a gym in our home that's

so accessible. Often, after the kids are tucked away,

we get into the spa and take a hot shower. It can be

very sexy after an intense workout.

e in a room

that is alive because

of the people in it.

Be in a room

that is alive because

of the people

who used to be in it.

Be in a room

that is alive because

of the people

who want to be in it.

Be in a room

that is alive because

of people who are there

who can no longer be seen.

Be in a room

that is alive because

of people who see those

who cannot be seen.

Be in a room like this. It makes you come alive!

*T*his is my luxurious and glamourous bedroom. I love it! I could just live here. In fact, I do. The rest of my house has no furniture.

*W*hether we are reading a great book, playing music
or making a beautiful baby, this room is a great place to let our hair down . . .

his is the library and it's my favorite because it has the stereo,

the HI-FI, CD, VCR, TV, the Los Angeles *and* New York Times

theatre sections, our hung Hirschfelds, Chan's framed straight-A

report card and Charles' desk and phone so I can listen to business.

MOOSE ("EDDIE")

My dog house is my favorite place to escape during my frantic filming

schedule. Once inside, I totally relax, whether it's playing with my toys,

snacking, taking a nap in the loft or lounging on the roof enjoying the view.

But most of all, I don't have to contend with any neurotic psychiatrist kicking me

off the furniture!

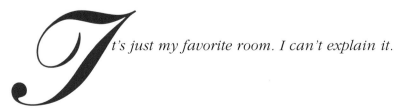

It's just my favorite room. I can't explain it.

*R*omance is what we love and our dining room sets the mood perfectly. The trees, candles and beautiful lighting make it so romantic. We dine and talk about how blessed we are and how much we love each other. Eating out is great, but dining in with friends, family or just the two of us is wonderful.

*W*e start every Sunday here with the New York / Los Angeles Times. *My son David brings the bagels. That's one way to get him over here.*

Opening the French doors that surround us lets the outside in. A roaring fire in the evening is magical. You could die from it.

 *irst of all our son*

Zack sprang from here.

So there's that.

If we had a kitchen in the

bedroom we'd never leave it.

It's a happening room.

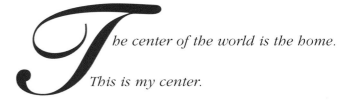

The center of the world is the home.

This is my center.

*P*lant a seed,

water it and nurture it.

It grows into life,

breathing beauty,

simplicity and peace.

This is why I love

the garden, the earth.

This is probably the best photo representation of my favorite little room for more than a few reasons. It features the elevated fireplace glow that radiates and engages the comfy couch corner around which we've cleared up about two zillion family storms. It includes the gratifying Cape Cod entryway we all love so much, and, Lord be praised, Marty cleaned up all his papers for the picture.

*O*ur favorite room at home has to be the kitchen / breakfast area. We really love its English country charm and warm cozy feeling. It's a great place for us to work or just "hang" with friends. There's a peaceful view across the gardens toward the pool that we really enjoy and find very romantic. It's a serene departure from our very hectic touring schedule.

 *t's like no other space we know.*

Index

ALLEN, RICK pg. 131
    Interior Designer: Kathryn McEachern, ASID
    Stylist: Jim Walters
    Hair & Make-up: David Miramontes

ANN-MARGRET pg. 27
    B&W Photo: Harry Langdon
    Interior Designer: Jerry Miller
    Stylist: Marlena Dictor

ANTON, SUSAN pg. 23
    Stylist: Marlena Dictor
    Hair & Make-up: Bridgett Ballou

BAIN, BARBARA pg. 81
    Interior Designer: Lenny Steinberg
        Dedicated to Bo Huston
    Hair & Make-up: Karen Scales
        Carrey Gibbons

BARKER, CLIVE pg. 57
    Stylist: Jim Walters

CAGE, NICOLAS pg. 87
    Interior Designer: Jerry Jackson
    Stylist: Jim Walters

CHANNING, CAROL pg. 113
    Stylist: Kristine Silverman

COMANECI, NADIA pg. 25
    Assistant: Rick Stockwell
    Stylist: Marlena Dictor

CONNER, BART pg. 25
    Assistant: Rick Stockwell
    Stylist: Marlena Dictor

DERN, LAURA pg. 69
    Stylist: Marlena Dictor
    Hair & Make-up: Karen Scales

DILLER, PHYLLIS pg. 21
    Stylist: Marlena Dictor

DUNCAN, SANDY pg. 31
    Stylist: Kimber Klusman
    Hair: David Siebenaler

"EDDIE", MOOSE pg. 115
    Assistant: Erick Huff
    Stylists: Art Gray

EDEN, BARBARA pg. 53
    Assistant: Rick Stockwell
    Stylist: Jim Walters
    Hair & Make-up: David Miramontes

ELVIRA pg. 39
    B&W Photo: Aaron Rappaport
    Stylist: Marlena Dictor

ETHERIDGE, MELISSA pg. 61
    Stylist: Marlena Dictor
    Hair & Make-up: Carrey Gibbons
        Karen Scales

FARENTINO, JAMES pg. 125
    Stylist: Marlena Dictor
    Hair & Make-up: Karen Scales

FUNICELLO, ANNETTE pg. 89
    Stylist: Jim Walters

G, KENNY pg. 111
    Interior Designer: Lyndie G Benson
    Assistant: David Burnham
    Stylist: Marlena Dictor
    Hair & Make-up: Carrey Gibbons

GARR, TERI pg. 109
    Interior Designer: Linda Marder
    Stylist: Marlena Dictor
    Hair & Make-up: David Miramontes

GEHRY, FRANK pg. 117
    Stylist: Marlena Dictor

GIBBONS, LEEZA pg. 19
Stylist: Marlena Dictor

GOLDBLUM, JEFF pg. 71
Stylist: Jim Walters
Make-up: Karen Scales
Hair: Frida Aradottir

GRAY, LINDA pg. 59
Assistants: Erick Huff, Ken Howard
Stylist: Jim Walters
Hair: Patrick Jagaille
Make-up: Jeannia Robinette

HALL, DEIDRE pg. 97
Stylist: Jim Walters

HAMLIN, HARRY pg. 99
Stylist: Brian Toffoli

HARTLEY, MARIETTE pg. 95
Assistants: Erin Mahon, Alex Bergnon
Stylist: Marlena Dictor
Hair & Make-up: David Miramontes

HATCHER, TERI pg. 127
Assistants: Erick Huff, Greg Carlson
Stylist: Marlena Dictor
Hair & Make-up: Bridgett Ballou

HAYS, ROBERT pg. 55
Stylist: Marlena Dictor
Hair & Make-up: David Miramontes

JACKSON, MARK pg. 119
Stylist: Kristine Silverman
Make-up: David Miramontes

JENNER, BRUCE pg. 105
Architect: Behshad Shokouhi
Interior Designer: Nancy Whaley
Stylist: Marlena Dictor
Hair & Make-up: Bridgett Ballou

JONES, SHIRLEY pg. 129
Stylist: Jim Walters

KELLERMAN, SALLY pg. 35
Stylist: Marlena Dictor
Hair & Make-up: David Miramontes

LAMPLEY, JIM pg. 63
Stylist: Marlena Dictor

LEACHMAN, CLORIS pg. 65
Stylist: Marlena Dictor
Hair & Make-up: David Miramontes

LEE, MICHELE pg. 121
Stylist: Marlena Dictor

LIGHT, JUDITH pg. 37
Interior Designer: Kathryn McEachern, ASID
Assistant: Erin Mahon
Stylist: Jim Walters
Make-up: David Miramontes

MacLAINE, SHIRLEY pg. 107
B&W: Ian Miles
Stylist: Marlena Dictor

MANCINI, HENRY pg. 29
Interior Design: Laura Mako
                Peter Choate

MANDEL, HOWIE pg. 101
Stylist: Jim Walters
Mural Artist: Nancy Bokash

MANILOW, BARRY pg. 47
Stylist: Marlena Dictor

MARSHALL, GARRY pg. 77
Interior Designer: Lil Chain, ASID

MARSHALL, PENNY pg. 75
Interior Designer: Werner Mayes
Hair & Make-up: Nadia Taricco

MASON, MARSHA pg. 73
    Stylist: Marlena Dictor
    Hair & Make-up: Elizabeth Dahl

MATHIS, JOHNNY pg. 15
    B&W: David Vance
    Stylist: Brian Toffoli

MATLIN, MARLEE pg. 45
    Interior Designer: Pia Grönning
    Stylist: Marlena Dictor
    Hair & Make-up: David Miramontes

McCLANAHAN, RUE pg. 41
    Stylist: Marlena Dictor
    Hair & Make-up: David Miramontes

MILLS, DONNA pg. 79
    Stylist: Jim Walters
    Hair & Make-up: Bridgett Ballou

MOORE, DEMI pg. 17
    Interior Designer: Linda Marder
    Stylist: Marlena Dictor
    Hair: Enzo Angileri
    Make-up: Carol Shaw

PESCOW, DONNA pg. 49
    Stylist: Kristine Silverman
    Hair & Make-up: David Miramontes

REYNOLDS, DEBBIE pg. 103
    Stylist: Kristine Silverman

ROSEANNE, pg. 91
    Interior Designers: Stacy Light/HTS
               Architectural Design
               Tracy Stultz, ASID
    Assistant: Barbara Benvil
    Stylist: Marlena Dictor

SALDANA, THERESA pg. 93
    Stylist: Kristine Silverman
    Hair & Make-up: Darin Walter

SHACKELFORD, TED pg. 67
    Interior Designer: Susan Rae Heinz
    Stylist: Marlena Dictor

SIMPSON, BART pg. 83
    Artist: Matt Groening

SOMERS, SUZANNE pg. 33
    Stylist: Jim Walters
    Hair: David Siebenaler

TIEGS, CHERYL pg. 123
    Interior Designer: Catherine Sodi/
               Judy Wilder Interiors
    Stylist: Marlena Dictor
    Hair & Make-up: David Siebenaler

TRAVOLTA, JOHN pg. 133
    B&W Photo: Robert Trachtenberg
    Stylist: Jim Walters

WALKER, BREE pg. 63
    Stylist: Marlena Dictor

WARREN, LESLEY ANN pg. 51
    Assistants: Rick Stockwell
    Wardrobe: Kurt Hessler
    Stylist: Marlena Dictor
    Hair & Make-up: David Miramontes

WARWICK, DIONNE pg. 85
    Stylist: Jim Walters

WILLIAMSON, MARIANNE pg. 43
    Interior Design: Beth Spivak
    Stylist: Marlena Dictor
    Hair & Make-up: Carrey Gibbons

COVER: The home of Carl Romeo &
            Tom Swale.

In benefit of

L.A. SHANTI

A non-profit organization that provides free emotional

support, counseling and education to people

affected by HIV, AIDS and other life-threatening illnesses.

Founded in 1983 by a group of dedicated volunteers,

L.A. Shanti was the first organization in Southern California

to provide direct services to people with AIDS.

L.A. Shanti has helped more than 50,000 people.

"At Shanti, caring works."

In benefit of

City of Hope

The City of Hope National Medical Center

and Beckman Research Institute is

renowned not only for its groundbreaking AIDS

research, but also for its work with leukemia

and other forms of cancer, diabetes and Alzheimer's disease.

*Our creed **"there is no profit in curing the body***

if in the process we destroy the soul"

defines the City of Hope's 83-year history of treating

the whole person, not just the disease.